BRAD PITT

by
Jill C. Wheeler

Visit us at
www.abdopub.com

Published by ABDO & Daughters, an imprint of ABDO
Publishing Company, 4940 Viking Drive, Edina, MN 55435.
Copyright ©2003 by Abdo Consulting Group, Inc.
International copyrights reserved in all countries. No part of
this book may be reproduced in any form without written
permission from the publisher.

Printed in the United States.

Graphic Design: John Hamilton
Cover Design: Mighty Media
Cover photo: Corbis
Interior photos: AP/Wide World, p. 1, 13, 14-15, 17, 18, 27,
43, 44-45, 48-49, 59, 62
    Corbis, p. 5, 9, 10, 21, 23, 24, 29, 30, 33, 34, 36, 39, 40,
       47, 51, 53, 54, 57, 60-61
    Dreamworks, SKG, p. 55
    MGM, p. 32
    Tristar Pictures, p. 41
    20th Century Fox, p. 50

Library of Congress Cataloging-in-Publication Data

Wheeler, Jill C., 1964-
    Brad Pitt / Jill C. Wheeler.
        p. cm. — (Star tracks)
    Includes index.
    Summary: Focuses on the personal life and television
and film acting career of Brad Pitt.
    ISBN 1-57765-769-1
       1. Pitt, Brad, 1963- —Juvenile literature. 2. Motion
picture actors and actresses—United States—Biography—
Juvenile literature. [1. Pitt, Brad, 1963- 2. Actors and
actresses.] I. Title. II. Series.

PN2287.P54 W49 2002
791.43'028'092—dc21
[B]
                              2001046147

CONTENTS

MEET

MR. EVERYMAN

THE RESIDENTS OF SPRINGFIELD, MISSOURI, were excited. One of their own had made it big in Hollywood. Now he was home to mark the opening of his latest movie. It was called *Meet Joe Black*.

The star had offered the movie premiere as a fundraiser. Springfield residents got to see the movie before anyone else—even people in New York City and Los Angeles. Proceeds from ticket sales were given to local charities. When the event was over, it had raised $66,000. The money was distributed to several local organizations that help young people.

The local media interviewed the star while he was in town for the fundraiser. Unlike many celebrities, Brad Pitt didn't claim to be a star. He said he's just a guy who makes movies. He also said it had been hard to go from Springfield, Missouri, to Hollywood, California, without losing his grasp on reality.

Despite multimillion dollar movie contracts and hordes of adoring fans, Brad Pitt has stuck pretty close to the goofy, fun-loving guy he was when he left Missouri for Tinseltown. "Brad never complains," said Julia Roberts, who starred with him in *The Mexican*. "If I had to describe him in two words, I'd say sunny disposition. He radiates it to everyone around him."

Unlike many other stars of his status, Pitt doesn't claim to be perfect. "My stuff to this stage has been very hit and miss," he admitted. "I certainly have my moments, but there's a giving up completely to the part, which I've only felt a few times. There's a focus I lack, at times."

Most fans haven't noticed any lack of focus. Pitt continues to be among the most popular stars in Hollywood. He also continues to marvel at the mechanics of stardom, which he sometimes finds a bit silly.

"I know when I go outside there will be one or two vans and they'll follow us four out of seven days a week," he said of the almost constant pressure from celebrity photographers. "I know that they're just wasting their day, so it doesn't bother me. It used to feel like such an invasion, and now it just feels like they're doing their thing and I'm doing my thing."

"It was just a confusing, confusing time," he added, speaking about the time he first appeared in the public eye. "And it's still confusing. People are telling you that you're much better than you certainly feel and people are saying you're much worse than you certainly are. And you're just trying to find out who… you are."

Brad Pitt during the filming of The Devil's Own.

MIDWESTERN
BOYHOOD

WILLIAM BRADLEY PITT WAS BORN ON December 18, 1963, in Shawnee, Oklahoma. He was the first child born to Bill and Jane Pitt. Bill worked as a trucker, and Jane was a family counselor. Shortly after Brad was born, Bill received a better job offer. To take it, the young family had to move to Springfield, Missouri.

When Brad was three, his parents had another son, Douglas. Two years later, they had a daughter, Julie. The three Pitt children grew up in a loving, supportive family. To this day, Brad calls his parents "the biggest guides in my life." Brad remembers his mother as the person who first believed he had talent. People who know the Pitt family say Brad looks like his father and acts like his down-to-earth mother.

If family came first for Brad, movies came a close second.

If there was a shadow in Brad's early years, it was his father's demanding career. Bill's strong work ethic made a big impression on his children. "My father spent thirty-six years, six days a week on the job," Brad said. Although Brad's father was often away from home, he did his best to spend time with his kids. The family often went on trips in the mountains or to the drive-in movie theater. The Pitts also saw that their children attended church regularly and learned right from wrong.

Brad and his brother, Doug, were like many siblings. While they loved each other, they also loved to tease each other. "I used to terrorize the kid," Brad admitted. "I'd lock him outside naked. I'd make him go get things and I'd time him. I'd say, 'If you can make it by twenty . . .' And then, just as he was running down the stairs I'd say, 'Twenty-one. Aw, too bad. I woulda' given you a prize.' "

If family came first for Brad, movies came a close second. "I was always in the movie theaters," he said. "I'd go to apethons. They'd show five movies back to back, all the ape movies, *Planet of the Apes*. That was the best."

Some of those movies made a big impression on young Brad. "When I was sitting there in my little backyard, playing with my puppy or whatever, eating Twinkies and drinking Kool-Aid, I'd dream of fame. . . Flicks like *Ordinary People* and *[One Flew Over the] Cuckoo's Nest*, they move you and shape you and I want to be a part of that."

At other times, Brad dreamed of being a musician or an artist. He took guitar lessons and often made sketches in a notebook he carried with him. He took parts in school plays and musicals, though he wasn't serious about it.

At Kickapoo High School, Brad was popular and a good student. He played team sports and was involved in student government and the debate team. But like many young boys, Brad also got into his share of trouble. "A lot of school is what you can get away with," he said. "I threw a book at a teacher once," he said of an argument he had with one of his teachers. "I didn't throw it hard, but it was a big book."

Brad played on the school's tennis team. Sometimes his competitive spirit got in the way. Once, he became very angry during a match and threw his racket on the ground. His father walked onto the court between games and said, "Are you having fun?" Brad told him no, he wasn't. So his father said, "Then don't do it," and walked away.

Brad never forgot the exchange. He knew his father could have punished him for his bad behavior. Instead, he used the incident to give Brad advice.

Of course, Brad was popular with the girls from a young age. He said he had his first kiss in fourth grade and his first girlfriend in junior high. He went steady with another girl through high school. They broke up when high school ended and both moved on. For Brad, the next new horizon was college.

Brad Pitt at the premiere of Meet Joe Black.

COLLEGE
HUNK

BRAD HAD GOOD GRADES, SO GOING TO college was not a question for him. The question was, which college? He chose to attend the University of Missouri at Columbia, where he planned to study journalism and advertising. It was only about 150 miles from Springfield. So in the fall after high school, he packed up his car and drove to Columbia.

Brad soon became a popular student at college, too. The now six-foot-tall blond, blue-eyed student posed shirtless for the school's annual calendar. The calendar quickly sold out and brought Brad to the attention of virtually the entire campus. He joined the Sigma Chi fraternity as well. "It was incredible to just get away from home, living with a bunch of guys," he said. "We had this idea of *Animal House*. And there was definitely that aspect. It was a highlight, without a doubt. Then, like everything, you grow out of it."

Brad did study journalism and advertising. For a time, he thought he might become an advertising art director. However, he disagreed with his teachers on many things. "They wanted the straight thing and it was really boring," he said. He ended up dropping out of college in 1986, just two credits shy of his degree. He didn't tell his parents that he

hadn't actually graduated because he didn't want them to worry.

"You don't really get it into your head that you can leave," he said. "Not too many people leave. It was about time to graduate and it just dawned on me—I can leave. It would be so simple, so easy. You load up the car, you point it west, and you leave. And everything's open."

Brad's next move was a dream come true. While he'd always loved movies, he'd never seriously thought he could be a part of that world. He explained it this way: "I thought, 'If I'd been born in California, I'd have a shot at them.' Then you realize you can go there."

At the end of his college career, Brad was driving a beat-up silver Datsun he called Runaround Sue. Just before graduation, Brad told his parents that he was heading west to study at the Art Center College of Design in Pasadena, California.

"I had my luggage high up to the back of my head and all the way to the top on the passenger side, so that I couldn't see behind me and just had a little room to shift," Brad said. "My philosophy was, all I need to see is forward. I'm heading west and that's all I need to see." So with his things packed and his parents' minds at ease, Brad pointed Runaround Sue west. He took off with the intention of becoming an actor.

STARTING
FROM
SCRATCH

PITT RECALLS HIS ARRIVAL IN HOLLYWOOD as less than climactic. "I remember being so excited as I passed each state line," he said. Before that point, he'd never been farther west than Wichita, Kansas. "I drove in through Burbank, and the smog was so thick that it seemed just like fog. I pulled in and went to McDonald's, and that was it. I just thought, shouldn't there be a little more?"

Pitt had no idea where to begin his quest for acting work. He had less than $400 to his name, so he moved into a two-bedroom apartment in North Hollywood along with eight other aspiring actors. "Two guys in the back room, two guys in the front room, four guys crashed out in the main room," Pitt recalled. "No furniture. We all had our little corners, with our little books stacked, our little clothes folded, our little sheets. A little cockroach motel by the bed as a safety measure. We shared an answering machine."

Pitt took on a series of odd jobs to make enough money to buy food and pay his bills. He delivered refrigerators to college dorm rooms. He worked as a telemarketer for three days. However, he was fired because he ended up chatting with the people he called instead of selling them anything. He also drove a limousine, and once even dressed up as a giant chicken to greet customers at a fast-food restaurant.

Pitt eventually landed a part in a movie as an extra. "I remember being an extra in *Less Than Zero*," he recalled. "I got to stand in the doorway during a party. I wore a pink-and-white striped tank top and sunglasses. I got paid 38 bucks." It wasn't much, but it fueled his desire even more.

In the meantime, the odd jobs allowed him to not only pay his bills, but also to meet people. One of the people he met steered him to an acting school where he could learn the basics of the craft. He studied for awhile with acting coach Roy London. Pitt said he feels fortunate that he got into a reputable acting school. "I got into a good acting class within the first three months, which is amazing," he said. "There are so many rip-offs out here . . . They're messing with people's dreams and making money off them. It makes me mad, because I was one of those people."

Pitt felt fortunate to get into a reputable acting school.

Pitt soon
learned to get
over his
intimidation
and do the best
he could.

At the school, Pitt met an aspiring actress who asked him to go on an audition with her in front of a talent agent. He did, and the rest is Hollywood history. "She asked me if I'd do the scene we prepared for class in front of all these agents," he recalled. "I said, 'Yeah, I guess so, whatever.' Boom. I got signed." The agent signed Pitt, instead of his friend.

With an agent, Pitt began to get into bigger and better auditions. He knew he was getting a little closer to his dream, but it was also nerve-racking. "Here I am, sitting in all these audition rooms, and I'm seeing these people who I've watched on TV or in films my whole life, and I'm intimidated," he said. He soon learned to get over his intimidation and do the best he could.

Within a month of getting an agent, Pitt landed a small part on the TV show *Dallas*. With a real job at last, he called home and confessed to his parents that he wasn't really studying graphic design. His father replied, "Yeah, I thought so."

HARD-
WORKING

A C T O R

PITT PLAYED A SMALL ROLE ON *DALLAS* for half a season. His charm and good looks quickly landed him in several teen magazines. He also got his first taste of the lack of privacy that comes with being famous. Tabloid newspapers began reporting a romance between Pitt and his *Dallas* costar, Shalane McCall. It would be the first of many times that Pitt was linked romantically with his costars.

Following *Dallas*, Pitt appeared in the daytime drama *Another World*. He followed that with appearances on episodes of TV shows *Growing Pains*, *Head of the Class*, *thirtysomething,* and *21 Jump Street*. In 1989, he made it to the big screen in the low-budget teen slasher film *Cutting Class*. Pitt himself called it an awful film. Still, it was work. He learned more with each job, and with each job he met more people.

Many of those people were impressed with the young actor from Missouri. "He caused such a stir on the set," recalled the directors of *thirtysomething*. "He was so good looking and so charismatic and such a sweet guy, everybody knew he was going places."

About 1990, Pitt landed a spot in a pilot for a new TV series by FOX called *Glory Days*, or *The Kids Are All Right*. He ended up acting in all six episodes of the short-lived series.

Pitt's next job was a part in the HBO movie *The Image*. That part led to a role in the series *Tales from the Crypt*, along with roles in B-movies *A Stoning in Fulham County* and *Happy Together*. Pitt was now getting steady work, although he wanted more serious roles. Still, he was acting, and doing what he wanted to do. Between jobs, he volunteered as a counselor, working with young people at a Los Angeles shelter.

Pitt switched acting gears slightly to appear in a television ad for Levi's jeans. The ad highlighted his all-American good looks. But he was anything but the all-American boy in his next part. In the TV-movie *Too Young To Die?*, he played a drug-addict who gets involved with a lost teenage girl.

Everybody knew
Pitt was going
places.

Pitt's character eventually convinces the girl to kill her former boyfriend. Pitt had to walk a fine line in the movie. He had to be evil enough to get costar Juliette Lewis to commit murder. Yet he also had to be charming enough to maintain his hold over her emotions.

Too Young To Die? was a turning point for both Pitt and Lewis. The two became romantically involved immediately after filming. The relationship would last for the next three years. The film also brought them to the attention of some influential people in Hollywood.

Lewis went on to receive an Academy Award nomination for her role in the feature film *Cape Fear*. Pitt took a part in the B-movie *Across the Tracks*. He played a track star in the piece, which costarred Rick Schroeder. Though it was a poor-quality film, Pitt made the most of it. It was his largest part so far, and it allowed him to carry a role as a serious actor, rather than just a pretty face.

By now, Pitt had called Hollywood home for about five years. He'd built up a credible résumé of movie and TV roles. He wasn't yet living his dream, but he could see it from there. "I hear people gripe all the time about coming to L.A. and not being taken seriously," he said. "You've gotta show 'em." Little by little, Pitt was doing just that.

J.D.

IN 1991, DIRECTOR RIDLEY SCOTT DECIDED
to take on a new project. It was to be a female buddy
film. Many male buddy films had been made, but no
one had done a female version. Scott cast stars
Susan Sarandon and Geena Davis to play the leads.
In *Thelma & Louise*, the characters leave home on a
weekend trip and end up on a crime-filled trip to
Mexico.

At one point, the women pick up a hitchhiker
named J.D., who later steals their money. Scott

originally cast William
Baldwin in the role. Then
Baldwin had the chance for a
bigger role in *Backdraft*.
Scott needed a new J.D. He
found the perfect one in Brad
Pitt. Pitt's good looks and
southern charm were perfect
for the J.D. character. Though he was only on screen
for about 15 minutes, his whirlwind romance with
Davis's character made him an immediate sensation.

Brad Pitt waves to fans at the 1999 Venice Film Festival.

Following the success of *Thelma & Louise*, Pitt knew he had to choose his next projects carefully. He didn't want to be typecast as just a handsome face with no talent. He chose to star in the comedy *The Favor* with Elizabeth McGovern. The movie didn't turn out as planned. In fact, it was never released in theaters. It only came out on video in 1994, when Pitt's fame had begun to grow.

Following *The Favor*, Pitt played the title role in *Johnny Suede*. The quirky movie was about a would-be rock star. It was a challenging role. Johnny, with his six-inch tall pompadour, had to be played just right. He had to be genuine enough so as not to appear ridiculous. Pitt pulled it off. One reviewer said Pitt's performance was the only thing that made the movie worthwhile.

Pitt followed those films with *Cool World*. Once again, it was a special challenge. Pitt had to act twice as much. First, he had to act like his character. Second, *Cool World* featured live actors interacting with animated characters. Computer technicians added the animation after the live actor's parts were filmed. So, while filming his part, Pitt had to act as if the animated characters were there with him even though they had not yet been added. The challenges proved to be too much. The film received poor reviews, and never caught on with audiences.

Everything changed with his next effort. Hollywood legend Robert Redford was preparing to direct a movie based on the popular book, *A River Runs Through It*. He asked Pitt to play the role of the younger brother. Pitt jumped at the chance to work with Redford in a serious role. He even learned how to fly-fish for the part, casting from the roofs of Hollywood buildings.

A River Runs Through It was a critical and popular success. Most everyone who saw it agreed Pitt was star material. But Pitt was always on the lookout for more challenging roles. For his next role, in *Kalifornia*, he played serial killer Early Grayce.

Pitt gained 20 pounds and let his hair and beard grow long and greasy for the part. His costar was his own real-life girlfriend, Juliette Lewis. Most people found *Kalifornia* too dark and frightening. Yet critics had to admit Pitt did a fine job playing the evil Grayce. Following *Kalifornia*, Pitt and Lewis broke up. Pitt's next job was a small comedic part in the film *True Romance*.

INTERVIEW
WITH A
STAR

AFTER A SHORT BREAK, PITT'S AGENT gave him two scripts to read. One was for a western called *Legends of the Fall*. Pitt had been asked to play the middle of three sons in the epic film. Edward Zwick and Marshall Herskovits, who worked on *thirtysomething,* were producing it. They remembered Pitt's work and wanted him back.

The other script was for the movie version of the popular book *Interview with the Vampire.* Director Neil Jordan had specifically requested Pitt for the part. "I saw everything he's done and he is just absolutely captivating," Jordan said. He wanted Pitt for the character of Louis Pointe du Lac, a Louisiana plantation owner who's been turned into a vampire.

Brad Pitt signing autographs at the 1999 Venice Film Festival.

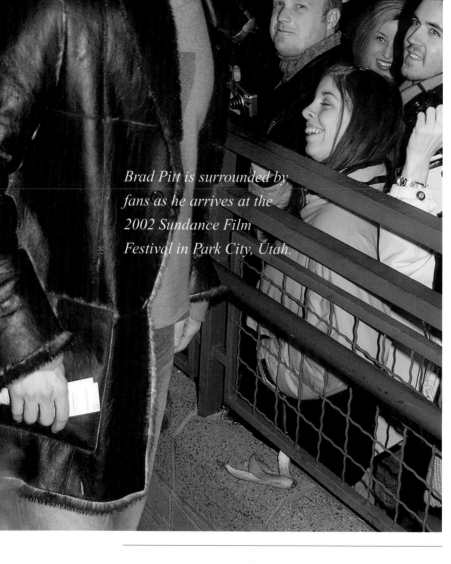

Brad Pitt is surrounded by fans as he arrives at the 2002 Sundance Film Festival in Park City, Utah.

Pitt accepted both parts. He flew to the Canadian Rocky Mountains to begin shooting *Legends of the Fall*. As soon as that shoot ended, he joined costar Tom Cruise to shoot *Interview with the Vampire*. Pitt's character made making the movie difficult. "I hated doing this movie," he said. "My character is depressed from the beginning to the end. Five and a half months of that is too much." Also, Anne Rice, the author who wrote the book on which the movie was based, criticized the casting. She thought both Cruise and Pitt were poor choices for the characters she had developed. In the end, she admitted the two actors did a good job.

The two movies were released within a few months of each other. By the time they came out, Pitt was exhausted. He also was the proud owner of a new home in Hollywood. *People* magazine had named him the "Sexiest Man Alive," encouraging his popularity.

Pitt quickly found out that being a movie star wasn't all glamour. He used to love to go to clubs and listen to music. Now he couldn't go out because everyone recognized him. He decided instead to try meeting other Hollywood celebrities. That turned out to be a disappointment as well. "I met a bunch of people," he said. "And it was that whole competitive, look-over, high-school-cafeteria thing. It was a shame."

Following his back-to-back successes, Pitt took off in yet another direction. He played a detective on the trail of a serial killer in *Seven*. While filming *Seven*, Pitt got to know costar Gwyneth Paltrow. They began dating after filming ended and became Hollywood's new hot couple.

Next, Pitt played a mental patient in *Twelve Monkeys*. He wasn't a shoo-in for the role. In fact, he had to work hard to convince director Terry Gilliam to take a chance and cast him. Gilliam took the chance. The result was an Academy Award nomination and a Golden Globe Award for Pitt for best supporting actor. For Pitt, it was another important victory. He was proving that he did not need his looks to succeed. He had talent.

*Brad Pitt and Gwyneth
Paltrow arrive at the
Academy Awards in Los
Angeles, March 25, 1996.*

Pitt's next role was in *Seven Years in Tibet*. He and the cast lived in South America's Andes Mountains, which doubled for the Himalaya Mountains, for five months while shooting the film. He also appeared in another thriller, *Sleepers*, and teamed up with actor Harrison Ford to play a member of the Irish Republican Army for *The Devil's Own*.

Brad Pitt starring in Seven Years in Tibet.

HITS
AND
MISSES

BY NOW, PITT'S SALARY HAD RISEN TO star-level as well. He is reported to have received $8 million for *Seven Years in Tibet*. In later films, that figure jumped to more than $17 million. Pitt earns a lot of money, but his Missouri roots help him keep it in perspective.

"It gets so crazy out there," he said. "People have no concept of money and the figures they offer can be crazy. I don't really know how I feel about it. Bottom line, are actors worth it? No, they're not. But if someone offers it to you are you going to say no? . . . There should always be a balance in salaries, they go up, they go down, but to me the important thing is the characters you're offered."

Pitt had worked steadily throughout his career. And like most actors, he'd had hits and misses. *Seven Years in Tibet* and his follow-up film, *Meet Joe Black*, where he plays the role of death, were misses. To make matters worse, in June 1997, while filming *Meet Joe Black*, Pitt broke up with girlfriend Gwyneth Paltrow.

Pitt took a short break to consider his next career move. He finally settled on yet another film that would test his limits as an actor. *Fight Club* was about a group of men who work in offices and fight each other at night for entertainment. Pitt played the leader of the group. Once again, it wasn't a glamorous role. He even had the caps on his front teeth chipped to better fit the part. *Fight Club* was released in 1999.

Pitt may have looked disturbed in *Fight Club*. Yet by that time, his personal life had taken a turn for the better. In 1998, Pitt's representative had set  him up on a date with *Friends* TV star Jennifer Aniston. The two hit it off immediately. But Pitt was cautious about going public with the relationship.

Once when dating Gwyneth Paltrow, photographers secretly took embarrassing photos of the two that ended up in a magazine and on the Internet. So for months after meeting, Pitt and Aniston tried to keep their relationship a secret. When the two finally admitted they were seeing each other, Pitt defended his earlier secrecy. "We just wanted to keep it special," he said. "Keep it ours."

Once the news was public, Pitt and Aniston didn't mind being seen together. They quickly became one of Hollywood's most romantic couples. It wasn't long before wedding rumors began to fly. Both stayed silent and kept on working.

*Brad Pitt and
Jennifer Aniston.*

FAIRY-TALE WEDDING, HOLLYWOOD STYLE

PITT SIGNED ON FOR TWO MORE MOVIES. One was a British flick called *Snatch,* directed by Guy Ritchie, who is married to Madonna. In *Snatch*, Pitt played an Irish Gypsy boxer. The part required him to learn a unique dialect of English that almost sounds like a foreign language.

The other was a romantic comedy costarring Julia Roberts called *The Mexican*. In *The Mexican*, Pitt played an errand boy for organized crime. One of his errands is to go to Mexico and retrieve a priceless antique revolver. Both *Snatch* and *The Mexican* did well in theaters, and Pitt was able to play parts he found both challenging and fun.

Brad Pitt and Jennifer Aniston at the 52nd Annual Emmy Awards in Los Angeles, September 10, 2000.

Brad Pitt and Jennifer Aniston arrive at the 59th Annual Golden Globe Awards *in Los Angeles, January 20, 2002.*

In the meantime, Pitt had been working on another special production. He and Aniston were planning their wedding.

Pitt and Aniston's wedding was among the most anticipated of the decade. The couple wanted a special, romantic wedding. They also wanted their privacy. Wedding staffers had to pledge to not

talk about the wedding to anyone. The couple also chose a location high on a bluff near Malibu for the July 29, 2000, ceremony.

Friends who attended the wedding said it mirrored Pitt and Aniston's

lightheartedness. In the vows, Aniston even promised to make Pitt's favorite banana milk shakes. There were also fireworks, four bands, 50,000 flowers, and a gospel choir. A guest told reporters, "It was an emotional service. It was not like a business thing. It was friends and family and celebration."

A HAPPY
HOMEBODY

PEOPLE WHO KNOW HIM WELL SAY PITT has remained down-to-earth despite his stardom. When a reporter from his hometown asked how he had adapted to the Hollywood lifestyle, he answered, "Lifestyle's what you choose. I have a good corps of friends out there. We just hang out and do what we did here. We barbecue. We go on road trips. It hasn't changed in that way." Pitt even likes to joke that in Springfield, Missouri, his brother, Doug, is the bigger celebrity.

Pitt stays close to his brother and the other members of his family. He purchased 600 acres of land in Missouri's Ozarks region so he could have a home away from Hollywood. He visits his parents nearly every Christmas. When he goes home, his mother even makes him do the grocery shopping.

Brad Pitt watches an NBA game between the Los Angeles Lakers and the Toronto Raptors.

In his spare time, Pitt enjoys music and collects guitars. He often sketches and has dabbled in architecture. He enjoys learning more about the works of architects Frank Lloyd Wright and Charles Rennie Mackintosh. Pitt even contributed photos to a book about the work of the Greene brothers, architects who pioneered the California Bungalow-style home in the early twentieth century. Lately, Pitt and Aniston have been restoring their Craftsman-style home in the hills of Hollywood.

Pitt likes to joke that when his fame runs out, he'll turn to architecture. "I'd like to design something like a city, or a museum." Speaking about fame, Pitt said, "You ride it as long as the trip lasts, then you go raise a family."

That fame hasn't worn off yet, however. Following *The Mexican*, Pitt went to work shooting a remake of the classic 1960 film *Ocean's Eleven*. He plays the part that Dean Martin played in the original. *Ocean's Eleven* is about a group of cool men who pull off a theft in Las Vegas, Nevada. Pitt also appeared in the thriller *Spy Game,* starring Robert Redford.

Brad Pitt's every man attitude plays into his thoughts about the future as well. "The only thing that life has taught me up to this point is that anything can happen," he said. "And everything can change at any given moment. Hey, listen, it's a work in progress. The truth is we're all works in progress until the day we go."

Brad Pitt and Jennifer Aniston at the premiere of Rock Star.

GLOSSARY

extra: an additional performer in a scene.

Irish Republican Army: a group dedicated to ending British rule in Ireland.

pompadour: a man's hairstyle where the hair is combed into a tall mound in the front.

WEB SITES

Would you like to learn more about Brad Pitt? Please visit **www.abdopub.com** to find up-to-date Web site links about Brad Pitt and his film career. These links are routinely monitored and updated to provide the most current information available.

INDEX